Mental Health, What's That?

Let's Explore: An Introduction to Mental Health for Children

Helping Kids Understand the Importance of Mental Health, and Connections between Their Mind, Body, and the World Around Them

Written by: Marcella K. Norman, MA   Illustrated by: Kenady Kitchen

Dedicated to my son, Kamryn, and my nieces:

McKinliegh,

Oliva,

Charli Rose,

Kaidence,

Cali,

~My godchildren

Joel,

Isir

May you live in a body that you understand, and in a world where you are seen, felt, and heard.

~My foremothers:

Kiziah,

Evelyn,

Millie,

Polly,

Dinnah,

Olivia,

Mable,

Katie,

Fanny B.,

Loretta,

Nanette,

THIS BOOK BELONGS TO:

_____

Mental health is a part of our overall well-being. Similar to our physical health, the effects of mental health are something we should be mindful of. It is important we learn about ways to take care of ourselves both physically and mentally. You may be wondering what mental health is. Let us start by exploring health overall.

Health refers to a person's mental or physical condition. A part of being healthy is taking care of our bodies. We take care of our bodies by eating healthy, exercising, getting enough sleep, practicing good hygiene, and being careful not to hurt ourselves. We can have good health or poor health. Good health is when we are at our best. Poor health is when we have sickness or disease in our bodies, poor hygiene, lack of sleep, or lack of proper nutrition. It is also important to know that some things that affect our health are out of our control.

With poor health, sometimes our bodies suffer from sickness. Sometimes, we have diseases, or we may get hurt. Our bones may become weak and break, or we can get bruised easily. Sometimes, we get sick because we come in contact with germs and do not take care of our hygiene. For instance, by not washing our hands we come in contact with germs that make us sick. Sometimes, we can have diseases that are incurable. When our health is poor, it is important we see a doctor to help us feel better and understand what is happening to our bodies.

We have explored some important details about health. Let us go over what we have learned so far. We learned that good health consists of taking care of our bodies, eating properly, getting enough sleep, and practicing good hygiene. We also learned that poor health consists of sickness in our bodies, lack of sleep, lack of nutrients, and sometimes getting hurt. When this happens, it is important to see a doctor. We also learned some diseases that affects us are incurable. Wow, we learned some great ways to take care of our bodies!

Is it possible for other parts of our bodies to need care? Does our brain need care? The answer is: Yes. Mental health is the well-being of our mind, which includes our thinking and the connection between our actions and feelings. "Mental Health" means a person's condition with regard to their mental and emotional well-being. Let us explore what mental health is.

Mental health impacts how we understand things and experience the world around us. It also affects how we make friends and build relationships. It affects our thought patterns and the way we feel about ourselves.

Like our physical health, mental health can be good or poor. Some examples of good mental health are when we feel good about ourselves, understand our feelings and are able to express them, and when our thought patterns are not harmful to us or others.

Some examples of poor mental health are when our thoughts seem worrisome or scary. Mental health can also be the cause when we cannot tell what is going on in our bodies, and why or when it is hard to converse with others or focus on a task. Poor mental health can sometimes show in the way we treat and think of ourselves. Sometimes there are things that affect us because we cannot control those things, such as our biology, our environment, poverty, lack of resources, and lack of safety.

Another important part of mental health is our emotions, also called our feelings. It is important for us to learn how to identify and understand our feelings and how they exist in our bodies. There are many emotions; and sometimes, it is hard to figure out what we are feeling.

It is important to know that no matter what emotion we are feeling, it is valid. That means no one can tell you what you are feeling or not feeling. Only you know that. It is okay to feel whatever emotion we are feeling. Emotions are not good or bad they just are. All emotions are okay and should be felt. Everyone has them. It is okay to feel emotions like anger, sadness, and grief. Sometimes, we can feel more than one emotion at the same time, and we do not have to choose one or the other. Learning how to identify emotions, and how they affect our body, can help us understand and express ourselves better. It is important to express our feelings and not keep them bottled up inside.

Emotions have a really big job to do. They can alert us of danger, and give our bodies warning when something is wrong. They all have their different functions, and this is why it is important to identify exactly what we are feeling. Let us explore some emotions, and their jobs.

Fear – Helps protect us from danger.

Happiness – Helps connect us with things that bring us enjoyment and make us feel good.

Anticipation – Shows us we are looking forward to something or planning.

Joy – Gives us a feeling of pleasure or happiness.

Surprise – Lets us know we are facing a new situation, something unexpected.

Anger – Is a natural response to threats; it encourages powerful, often aggressive, feelings and behaviors, which allow us to defend ourselves when we feel attacked. A certain amount of anger is necessary to our being.

Sadness – Helps us know something hurts us or hurts our feelings, and it is okay to feel that way.

Nervousness – Lets us know we are uncomfortable, and sometimes we may not feel safe.

Guilt – Lets us know we may have done something we think and feel was wrong.

Shame – This is an inward reflection of how we are feeling about our actions, when we sense we have done something unacceptable.

There are many more emotions. Explore and see how many emotions you can think of?

Our feelings, thoughts, and behaviors are all connected. Therefore, it is important to recognize what kind of thoughts we are having. A harmful thought can give you a bad feeling and cause you to respond badly, while positive thoughts make you feel good and act more positively.

One more very important part of mental health is trauma. Wow! Trauma is a big word. Let us explore what it means. Trauma is an emotional reaction to terrible events that happen in our lives. Trauma can affect our body and our mind. When we experience physical trauma reactions, it involves our body's response to threats , abuse, and serious injuries. Mental reactions to trauma, which are sometimes longer lasting may consist of terrifying thoughts , painful feelings, and triggers. "Triggers" can include sights , sounds, thoughts, or smells that remind us of the traumatic event in some way. Trauma can also affect us even when it has not directly impacted us. For example, you can also experience trauma when you hear about firsthand trauma of another person. This is called secondary trauma.

Traumatic experiences can include natural events like an earthquake or house fire. It can also include events like violence, death, serious accidents, war, attacks, abuse, and neglect. When we experience something traumatic, it can be very difficult for us to deal with. It will probably be something we have never dealt with before. We may not feel safe anymore, or feel like ourselves. We may question things we once believed, like our faith, and trust of others. It is important to know that everyone deals with trauma differently even if it is the same type of trauma. There is no right or wrong way to react to traumatic experiences. Sometimes, we heal on our own overtime with the help of our family and friends. Sometimes, it can have long-lasting effects and lead to more serious mental health issues ,and the need for professional help.

How can we tell the difference between mental health symptoms, and physical health symptoms? First, it is important to understand how physical health and mental health symptoms can seem alike. For example, think of how our heart beats very fast when we run. The same is true when we are nervous or scared. Our hearts can beat fast when we are scared. We can sweat and have trouble catching our breath. This is because both our physical health and mental health depend on our nervous system. The nervous system is like the boss of our body. It tells our brain and body what to do by sending messages through our nerves.

Explore and see what differences between mental and physical health you can identify?

thoughts
feelings
exercise
sleep
mind

Mental disorder, as with physical sickness, sometimes calls for a visit to a professional to figure out what is wrong with us. A disorder is another word for disease often used in mental health. Medical professionals are trained to treat our bodies. While mental health professionals are trained to treat our minds, sometimes both physical and mental health professionals may determine that we need medicines to help us feel better.

Medical professionals give us their expert advice on ways to take care of ourselves. Mental health professionals may suggest therapy. In therapy we may learn coping skills. Therapy is a safe space to talk about our feelings ,and the things that hurt us. A coping skill is something we do to help us manage difficult emotions. For example, these are some easy coping skills we can perform on our own:

- Exercise is good to help us feel better when we are bored, sad, or even mad.

- Taking deep breaths can help us when we feel frightened, nervous, or uncomfortable.

- Writing our feelings in a journal helps us express what we are feeling.

- Arts and crafts keep us busy.

- Talking to a friend or an adult about how we are feeling can help us feel heard.

- We can count to ten when we are angry and ask ourselves on a scale from one to ten how big our emotion is. If we are above a certain number, we can pause and do a preferred activity until we are feeling better.

- Asking for help from adults makes them know that we need them.

There are some things we can do to take care of both our mental and physical health. It is important to eat healthy, exercise, and go to the doctor when we are not feeling fine. We can talk to a professional when our thoughts and feelings are upsetting us, or when we get sick or hurt. A good way to tell when we need to see a professional for our mental health is when our thoughts and feelings make it hard for us to do the things we do every day, like get out of bed, play with friends, eat properly, or if we are not able to sleep.

Wow, we learned a lot about mental health! Most importantly, we learned that our mental health is just as important as our physical health. Speaking about mental health regularly will help us understand that we all may not experience mental illness, but everyone may have a period when their mental health is at risk, and that there is no shame in talking about it. It is important to know that it is okay to ask for help. Mental health is a part of our overall well-being.

FEELINGS CHART

Fear

Anticipation

Surprise

Sadness

Joy

Anger

Shame

Happiness

Nervous

Guilt

Glossary

Abuse – unfair, cruel, or violent treatment of somebody; for example, child abuse, sexual abuse, or emotional abuse.

Biology – can be defined as the science of life and living things and their evolution.

Children's mental disorder- mental disorders among children are described as serious changes in the way children typically learn, behave, or handle their emotions, which causes distress and problems getting through the day.
https://www.cdc.gov/childrensmentalhealth/symptoms.html

Cope – to deal with problems and difficult situations and try to come up with a solution.

Disease –an illness that affects a person, animal, or plant : a condition that prevents the body or mind from working normally.

Emotion – a strong feeling, such as love, anger, joy, hate, or fear.

Feeling – an emotional state or reaction.

Health – the condition of being well or free from disease; the overall condition of someone's body or mind.

Hygiene – conditions or practices (as of cleanliness) conducive to health.

Illness – a disease or a period of sickness affecting the body or the mind.

Incurable –(of a sick person or a disease) not able to be cured.

Infection – the state produced by the establishment of one or more pathogenic agents (such as a bacteria, protozoans, or viruses) in or on the body of a suitable host.

Mental – adjective, of or relating to the mind.

Mental health – an important part of overall health and well-being. Mental health includes our emotional, psychological, and social well-being. It affects how we think, feel, and act. It also helps determine how we handle stress, relate to others, and make healthy choices. Mental health is important at every stage of life, from childhood and adolescence through adulthood.

Mental illness – a health condition involving changes in emotion, thinking, or behavior (or a combination of these). Mental illnesses are associated with distress and/or problems functioning in social, work, or family activities.

Neglect – the ongoing failure to meet a child's basic needs and is the most common form of child abuse.

Nervous system – the system of nerves in your body that sends messages for controlling movement and feeling between the brain and the other parts of the body.

Nutrition – the act or process of nourishing or being nourished.

Physical – relating to the body as opposed to the mind.

Professional – a person engaged or qualified in a profession.

Psychotherapy-treatment of mental or emotional disorder or of related bodily ills by psychological means.

Resource – a source of supply or support, an available means.

Safety – the state of being protected from danger or harm.

Symptom- a mental or physical feature that indicates a condition of disease

Trauma – a mental or physical reaction caused by severe shock, especially when the harmful effects last for a long time.

Treat – give medical care or attention to; try to heal or cure.

National Crisis numbers :
National Suicide Prevention Hotline : 800-273-8255
Crisis Text line: Text HOME to :741741 to connect with a crisis counselor
24/7 , from anywhere in the United States.

For this book the following references works were used: The Chicago Manual of Style (CMS; 17th edition), Words Into Type (3rd edition), and Merriam-Webster's Collegiate Dictionary (11th edition, online).

ABOUT THE AUTHOR

Marcella Kamile Norman, MA, is a clinical psychotherapist who holds a bachelor's degree in psychology from Ashford University and a master's degree in counseling psychology from Rosemont College in Pennsylvania.

Her work began with the community health population and with those experiencing mental health challenges and some kind of psychosis. More recently, Marcella works with those dealing with substance abuse addictions in the drug and alcohol field.

Marcella has an extensive background in various disciplines in the mental health field. While working for a community-based mental health program, she realized that there was a great need for more African American clinician representation. So, she has dedicated herself to working with and for the African American community.

Marcella also is currently working with children experiencing mental health disorders such as attention deficit hyperactivity disorder (ADHD), anxiety, depression, trauma, and post-traumatic stress disorder (PTSD). This is her motivation and drive to impart psychoeducation through her published works, such as *Mental Health, What's That? Let's Explore: An Introduction to Mental Health for Children.*

She has also worked with the international community providing psychoeducation through workshops, specifically in Haiti. Marcella is currently pursuing licensure and continually seeking to expand her knowledge and service in the field of mental health, both in her community and internationally.

ACKNOWLEDGEMENTS

To Kamryn – Thanks for teaching me firsthand how important it is as a parent to take care of my mental health. You are my son- shine, always brightening my day!

To Mandy – Thank you for being supportive, and being there for me especially, when I am experiencing those really big emotions!

To Mom – You are my everything, my therapist, my comfort, my confidant, my sound board, and my life coach. I am so thankful I have you as a mother to help me through this big world!

To Dad – Thank you for being the strength and glue for our family, your love has helped me in more ways than I can count!

To Stephen – I have always admired your confidence and how you navigate the world, keep doing you bro!